CHINESE FESTIVALS

The Qingming Festival

Edited by Li Chaodong
Translated by Clair Yingping Yue

Books Beyond Boundaries
ROYAL COLLINS

Pure Brightness

Du Mu

It drizzles thick and fast on Pure
Brightness Day.
All mourners on the way are
heartbroken and in dismay.
Where can they find a tavern to
drown their sad hours?
A cowherd points at the village
amid apricot flowers.

Before Pure Brightness, although spring has arrived, the temperature is still low, and all things on earth haven't woken up from the cold and long winter. The land is still bleak and chilly.

Pure Brightness is between the Middle of Spring and Late Spring. It is an important climate dividing line which declares the arrival of the warm season of a new year.

Minor Cold
(January 5–7)

Winter Solstice
(December 21–23)

Major Snow
(December 6–8)

Minor Snow
(November 22–23)

Beginning of Winter
(November 7–8)

Frost's Descent
(October 23–24)

Cold Dew
(October 8–9)

Autumnal Equinox
(September 22–24)

White Dew
(September 7–9)

End of Heat
(August 22–24)

Sol

Rain Water (February 18–20)

Awakening of Insects (March 5–7)

Spring Equinox (March 20–21)

The Middle of Spring (the second month of the lunar calendar)

Pure Brightness (April 4–6)

Late Spring (the third month of the lunar calendar.)

Grain Rain (April 19–21)

Beginning of Summer (May 5–7)

Grain Buds (May 20–22)

Grain in Ear (June 5–7)

Summer Solstice (June 21–22)

Minor Heat (July 6–8)

4

rms

Pure Brightness falls between April 4 and April 6 every year, with April 5 being the most common day. It is the fifth solar term in a year. According to *Huainanzi · Astronomy* of the Western Han Dynasty (206 BC–AD 25), "the wind of Pure Brightness blows" "fifteen days after Spring Equinox."

Pure Brightness means the things growing in this period are clean, bright, and pure.

—*A Wide Record of the Fasti*

All things on earth growing currently are clean, bright, and pure, so we call it Pure Brightness.

—*One Hundred Questions about the Fasti*

After Pure Brightness, the weather is getting warmer, spring is coming back, and everything is waking up. It is the time suitable for spring plowing and sowing. It is said that "Before and after Pure Brightness, people plant melons and beans" and that "Pure Brightness is the best time for planting trees."

"The wind of the pear blossom blows just on Pure Brightness." Many kinds of fruit trees like pear, persimmon, jujube, citrus, ginkgo, and waxberry are in bloom at this time.

"Before Pure Brightness, tea leaf has a two-piece bud." The tea trees grow slowly before Pure Brightness and sprout limited pieces of bud. However, the tea buds are plump and jade green in color. After Pure Brightness, the weather gets warmer, and the tea trees grow into a flourishing period.

Pure Brightness is a very important time node for agriculture. Many crops which grow slowly begin to grow quickly at this time.

"On Pure Brightness, wheat grows three sections of the stem." Wheat in Northeast and Northwest China enters the jointing stage. In the south of the Huang-Huai region, wheat is entering the booting stage, and rape has been in the full-bloom stage. In the areas south of the lower reaches of the Yangtze River, people also begin to sow early-season and middle-season rice, as well as maize, sorghum, and cotton.

Jointing Stage

Booting Stage

MINI ENCYCLOPEDIA

What is jointing and booting?

Jointing means that the sections of the main stem grow quickly after crops like rice, wheat, sorghum, and maize have grown to a certain stage. After the jointing, the fruit portion on the top elongates rapidly, which is called booting.

By Pure Brightness, the temperature in most parts of China is above ten degrees, and it is warm and comfortable. But sometimes, the cold air is strong and can cause the cold wave to move southward, making many places in the South go through a short period of low temperatures and rainy weather. And this is what we call "Late Spring Coldness."

It drizzles thick and fast on Pure Brightness.

It is to be noted that the poem "Pure Brightness" by Du Mu only represents the scene of the middle and lower reaches of the Yangtze River Plain. China has a vast territory, and many places are not the same as what the poem describes. For example, in some places in the North, there is little or even no rain before and after Pure Brightness. Spring drought often happens in these places. At this time, we can really say that "the spring rain is as precious as oil."

Before and after Pure Brightness, animals regain their vitality and then are busy with their lifetime event. Many animals choose to breed in spring because of the suitable climate, and they can find many kinds of food. As a result, more baby animals can survive better. Animals need to make great efforts for breeding, such as the migration of birds and fish.

Some birds spend the winter in warm Southern areas and fly to the North to breed in spring. Then they will fly back to the South next winter with the grown-up chicks. These birds are called winter migrants.

In spring, the Yangtze River is warm, and the flow is gentle. Many fish will migrate with the sea tide to the Yangtze River to spawn. When baby fish grow up, they swim back to the sea on their own.

After a long period of evolution and development, we humans have a strong ability to withstand unfavorable climates and ensure food supply. So we can give birth to new lives all year round.

The baby conceived in spring can share with the mother the pleasant climate and plenty of food in the mother's belly. Being pregnant with a baby before and after Pure Brightness is a really happy thing.

The succession of humanity means blood lineage and responsibility. No matter how we spread genes and start a big family, we should not forget the roots deep in the ground, not forget where we come from and the source of civilization and life.

Xinzheng, Henan Province

Yellow Emperor Xuan Yuan

The Yellow Emperor was the tribal chief in early ancient China and unified various tribes at that time with his political and military achievements. He is one of the earliest leaders of the Chinese nation. The Yellow Emperor led our ancestors from barbarism to civilization, starting the splendid culture of the Chinese nation, so he is called the "Father of Chinese Culture."

For thousands of years, inspired by the same cultural gene, Chinese people have been coming to the Ye Mausoleum in Qiaoshan, Shaanxi Province, to visit the ancestral tomb and worship their ancestors. Every Qingming Festival, thousands of Chinese, both at home and abroad, gather at the Sacrifice Square in front of the Xuanyuan Palace to hold a grand ceremony to offer sacrifices to the Yellow Emperor and express their admiration and gratitude.

In 2006, the "Memorial Ceremony of the Yellow Emperor Mausoleum" was listed on the National Intangible Cultural Heritage list.

Qiaoshan, Shaanxi Province

When it comes to the family, we need to go to visit and sweep the tombs of our ancestors who have passed away, such as grandpa's grandparents and even earlier ancestors, to show respect and remembrance for them. Thanks to them, we have the chance to come to the world. The ancestor worship at the Qingming Festival helps us remember where the water is from when drinking and reminds us not to forget our roots.

As an important tradition of the Qingming Festival, ancestor worship is said to date back to the Zhou Dynasty (1046–256 BC), with a history of more than 2,500 years. At first, the nobles held ceremonies to offer sacrifices to heaven, earth, and ancestors in the Middle of Spring. Later, common people followed suit, and this custom gradually spread.

The Qingming Festival has now become a festival with great significance and rich connotations, which is also related to its combination with the Cold Food Festival.

The Cold Food Festival is said to be created in honor of
Jie Zitui, a loyal official of the Jin State in the Spring and
Autumn Period (770-476 BC). According to the legend,
Chong Er, the prince of the Jin State in the Spring and
Autumn Period, was persecuted and forced into exile in
other states. Jie Zitui was always together with Chong
Er and even "cut meat from his own leg to serve Chong
Er" when the prince was faint with hunger. This kind
of behavior is certainly a reluctant action of ancients in
distress, which should not be advocated and imitated.

Later, having endured untold hardship and suffering, Chong Er finally returned to Jin, ascended the throne, and became Duke Wen of Jin, one of the "Five Hegemons of the Spring and Autumn Period." He was determined to reward meritorious statesmen, thinking of Jie Zitui first. But Jie Zitui was indifferent to fame and wealth and didn't want to take credit and be rewarded. Carrying his mother on the back, he hid in the Mian Mountain.

Duke Wen of Jin sent people to search the Mian Mountain. Not finding Jie Zitui after several days of search, Duke Wen of Jin had no alternative but to give orders to set fire to the mountain, hoping to force Jie Zitui to come out. The fire burned for three days and nights. Duke Wen of Jin went up the mountain with other people to look for Jie Zitui, only to find Jie Zitui and his mother holding tightly a big willow tree and being burned to death together.

In order to commemorate Jie Zitui, Duke Wen of Jin buried the mother and son under the big willow tree and renamed Mian Mountain Jie Mountain. He also issued a decree to set the day when he set fire to the mountain as the Cold Food Festival. On this day, everyone was not only required to worship but was also forbidden to make a fire and was only allowed to eat cold food.

The following spring, Duke Wen of Jin and his officials climbed the mountain to offer sacrifices to Jie Zitui. To his surprise, the burned and bare Jie Mountain was full of life again, and the old willow tree was back from the dead with lush greenery swaying.

With an eyeful of the green, Duke Wen of Jin couldn't help exclaiming over the greatness of life. And the big willow tree swaying in the wind was like the graceful Jie Zitui walking towards him.

Some people also believe that the Cold Food Festival follows the custom of changing fire in ancient times. It is mentioned in *The Rites of Zhou* that in the Middle of Spring, the official in charge of fire would hold the muduo (bell with a wooden clapper) to announce the prohibition of fire to the whole country. It is dry in spring, so keeping kindling can easily cause a fire. Spring thunder can also result in a big fire.

At this time, the ancients often carried out a solemn sacrificial ceremony to extinguish the previous year's kindling, which is called "Prohibiting Fire." Then people drilled the wicker to make a new fire for the use of the next year, which is called "Changing Fire." Between Prohibiting Fire and Changing Fire, people could only eat cold food prepared in advance.

Making a new fire after the Cold Food Festival is a kind of transitional ceremony to bid farewell to the old and welcome the new. It not only reveals the message of the season changing but also symbolizes the beginning of new life and a new cycle, which is consistent with the idea of worshiping the ancestors and looking forward to the new life of the Qingming Festival.

More fundamentally, the Cold Food Festival was one or two days before the Qingming Festival and often lasted for several days until after the Qingming Festival. Worship activities were held at both two festivals. Hence gradually, they were merged.

Muduo

Although both the Qingming Festival and the Cold Food Festival had a long history, they did not become legal holidays until the Tang Dynasty (AD 618–907). At that time, many officials would return to their hometowns to visit and sweep tombs, which affected the work during the two festivals.

Emperor Xuanzong of the Tang Dynasty then issued a decree in the year of AD 736 announcing "a four-day holiday for the Cold Food and Qingming Festivals." In AD 777, the imperial court stipulated that "the Cold Food Festival together with the Qingming Festival shared a holiday of five days." By AD 790, two more days were added to the holiday. The officials and common people had a seven-day holiday to visit the tombs and offer sacrifices at ease.

In the Song Dynasty (AD 960–1279), there was also a holiday of seven days for the Cold Food and Qingming festivals. The tomb-sweeping activities around the Qingming Festival had also become a major event involving the whole society. Later, in the Yuan, Ming, and Qing dynasties (AD 1271–1912), although the Qingming Festival was no longer an official holiday, people still got around to offering sacrifices to their ancestors.

In 2008, the Qingming Festival became an official holiday again. With a vacation of three days, we can better go for an outing, visit the tombs, and worship our ancestors.

The tomb-sweeping activities usually take place in the countryside. After a long and dreary winter, people can finally take off their thick coats. After offering sacrifices to their ancestors, they go for an outing in the wild, breathing fresh air and changing their moods of sadness.

Children and their parents will fly kites, swing, kick the ball, and play with wickers. These are the common activities at the Qingming Festival.

(1) Flying Kites:
The ancients believed that the wind on Pure Brightness was suitable for flying kites. There is an old saying, "Flying kites on Pure Brightness." People wrote disasters and diseases on the kite and cut the kite line when the kite was flying high, letting it fly away with the wind. This symbolizes that illness and bad luck are taken away by the kite.

(2) Swing:
The earliest folk swinging activity was called "Qianqiu," later changed to "Qiuqian," becoming gradually the game played among girls. According to folk legend, swinging can help get rid of all diseases. The higher you swing, the better your life will be.

(3) Cuju:

"Cu" means kicking with the foot, and "Ju" means the leather ball. "Cuju" means kicking the ball with the foot, which is a football game in ancient times. Cuju is said to be originally created by the Yellow Emperor to train warriors.

(4) Insert or Wear Willow Branches:
There are three possible meanings. The first is to commemorate Shennong, the father of Chinese agriculture, the second is to exorcise evil spirits, and the third is to commemorate Jie Zitui.

The Qingtuan (green dumpling) is the most famous cold food during the Qingming Festival.

According to research, Qingtuan appeared no later than the Tang Dynasty. Every spring, families in the south of the Yangtze River will steam a lot of Qingtuan in advance for consumption around the Qingming Festival. Today, Qingtuan has become a kind of popular seasonal snack, and its function as a ritual food is gradually fading.

The skin of Qingtuan is made from glutinous rice flour mixed up with pulp wheat grass and wormwood juice. The red bean paste with lard is the most classic filling. The delicate fragrance and the agreeable sweetness really make people salivate just at the thought of it. Then do you know the detailed steps to make Qingtuan?

① ② ③ ④ ⑤ ⑥ ⑦ ⑧ ⑨

Aiban   It is also made from wormwood and is a necessary dish for the Hakka people at the Qingming Festival. A saying goes around that "People who eat Aiban around the Qingming Festival will not get sick all year round."

Sanzi   It was called "Hanju" in ancient times and is related to the Cold Food Festival. In many places, people have the custom of eating Sanzi at the Qingming Festival. Sanzi made in the North is often big and made from wheat, while in the South, Sanzi is often small, exquisite, and made from rice.

Zitui Mo (steamed bun)   It is said to be made by people in Shanxi Province to commemorate Jie Zitui and is also called Lao Momo (old-steamed bun). It looks like the warrior's helmet in ancient times in shape, with eggs and dried jujube fruits added inside and a cap on top. The bun is also decorated with various kinds of dough flowers.

Luosi (River Snail)   The meat of Luosi tastes rich and delicious before and after the Qingming Festival. There is a saying going on among farmers that "River snail on Pure Brightness is even better than a goose." When eating Luosi, people use a needle or toothpick to pick out the meat, which is called "Tiaoqing" and forms a nice match with "Taqing" (going for an outing).

In addition, there are various kinds of eating customs around the Qingming Festival in other parts of China, such as eating cold eggs (Shandong Province), cold pancakes rolled with bitter herbs (Tai'an, Shandong Province), red date cakes (the Northern areas), rice with leaf mustard (Wenzhou, Zhejiang Province), and green seed cakes (Chaoshan, Guangdong Province).

The Qingming Festival integrates the natural solar terms with cultural customs, reflecting the cultural tradition of the Chinese nation to remember with gratitude the ancestors and strive for new progress. It also reflects the persistent pursuit of harmonious coexistence between humans and nature. It is not only the grand ceremony for us to farewell to the old and welcome the new but also the most vivid interpretation of "the work for the year is best begun in spring."

CHINESE FESTIVALS

The Qingming Festival

Edited by Li Chaodong
Translated by Clair Yingping Yue

First published in 2023 by Royal Collins Publishing Group Inc.
Groupe Publication Royal Collins Inc.
BKM Royalcollins Publishers Private Limited

Headquarters: 550-555 boul. René-Lévesque O Montréal (Québec) H2Z1B1 Canada
India office: 805 Hemkunt House, 8th Floor, Rajendra Place, New Delhi 110 008

Original Edition © Hohai University Press

ISBN: 978-1-4878-1153-2

To find out more about our publications, please visit www.royalcollins.com.

ABOUT THE EDITOR

Li Chaodong, born in 1963, graduated from the Department of History of East China Normal University. He is a famous education publisher in China. He has edited and published more than 50 sets of books. He has won the title of "National Leading Talent in Press and Publication" and "China's Annual Publication Figure." He is the Founding Vice President of the All-China Federation of Industry and Commerce Book Industry Chamber of Commerce, Vice President of the Fifth Council of the Books and Periodicals Distribution Association of China, Vice Chairman of Anhui Publishing Association, and Vice Chairman of Jiangsu Publishing Association.